First Bible Stories

by
Lawrence Waddy

Illustrated by
Mark Mitchell

PAULIST PRESS
New York and Mahwah, N.J.

Library of Congress Cataloging-in-Publication Data

Waddy, Lawrence.
  First Bible stories/by Lawrence Waddy: illustrated by Mark Mitchell.
    p. cm.
  ISBN: 0-8091-6613-5 (pbk.)
  1. Bible stories, English. [1. Bible stories.] I. Mitchell, Mark. 1951– ill. II. Title.
BS551.2.W218 1994
220.9'505–dc20   93-34710
                                          CIP
                                          AC

Published by Paulist Press
997 Macarthur Boulevard
Mahwah, New Jersey 07430

Printed and bound in the
United States of America

Contents

JESUS AS TEACHER

JESUS AS HEALER

FOLLOWING JESUS ON THE ROAD TO JERUSALEM

Preface

*T*he purpose of this book is to open doors into the Bible.

Nowhere else in all of literature can you find such riches between the covers of a book as in the Bible; but young readers need to be introduced to it step by step.

These stories have been chosen to illustrate courage and faith, and the response by men and women to great challenges. It is my hope that young people reading and discussing the stories will be eager to open the door further and explore more of the Bible.

I would urge teachers and parents to keep an atlas close at hand while Bible stories are being read. Comparison of modern maps to maps of Bible lands produces surprises and stimulates interest. Did you know that Abraham came from Iraq? When God told Jonah to go to Nineveh, also in Iraq, he set out in the opposite direction, from Joppa (Jaffa now: can you find it?) toward Gibraltar. Jesus never made a journey of much more than a hundred miles. My experience is that eager young minds love to discover links like these.

Finally, I thank my grandchildren for listening to these stories and encouraging me to share them with you.

The Bible...In the Beginning

*T*here are hundreds of stories in the Bible. When you are older, hopefully you will look forward to reading more of them than just the ones included here.

For now, let's start at the beginning of the Bible. The earliest stories tell how God made the world. At first there was no life. Then plants and animals and birds and fish lived on the land and in the oceans and skies.

After many millions of years the first men and women came into being. They were like animals in most ways, but different because they knew right from wrong, and they could think about God.

Bible stories tell how men and women, starting with Adam and Eve, have looked for God and tried to find the way to live good lives. You can find out more about the people in these stories by reading the Bible passages that follow each story. Every book of the Bible—and every chapter in each book—will provide you with a new route to discovery.

Hebrew Scriptures

4

Noah

*O*ne of the first stories is about a terrible flood. Noah was a good man who prayed to God every day and listened to him. God warned Noah that it was going to rain and rain and rain.

"Build a boat for your family," God told him. "Make room for a pair of each of the animals, so that they will not all be drowned."

So Noah built a boat, which he called the Ark. Other people laughed at him.

"Why build a huge boat like that?" they asked. "You will never sail in it."

Then came the rain, more than anyone had ever seen. Houses were under water, and trees were carried away, while frightened people tried to climb high enough to be safe. Many of them were swept away by the swirling water.

Noah's Ark floated away on the huge sea which the flood had created. He had quickly collected two of each kind of animal, as God had commanded him. Now he tried to steer the boat. With him were his wife, his three sons, and their wives.

They floated and tossed on the water for forty days. Then at last the rain stopped. Noah sent a dove to look for dry land. Some time later the dove flew back with an olive twig in its beak. Noah knew from this that there must still be trees on dry land. Gradually the water began to recede, and Noah was able to let all of the animals out.

The Bible tells us that Noah's three sons—who were named Shem, Ham, and Japheth—went off in different directions, and became the ancestors of new nations.

Your route to discovery—Genesis 6:5-9

Abraham

*T*he history of the Hebrew people began with Abraham. He lived about two thousand years before Jesus. He came from a city called Ur, in the country which is now Iraq. It was a rich city, built along the banks of the river Euphrates.

It seems that Abraham and his father Terah were prosperous, but Abraham knew that God was calling him to a different life. In his heart he believed in one God, creator of all the world, not in the many gods of his native city.

Abraham and Terah left Ur with a caravan of family members and servants. First they journeyed up the river to Haran, where Terah died. Then God called Abraham to turn to the south. "Go to the land that I will show you, and I will make of you a great nation."

Abraham drove his flocks slowly toward Canaan, the land which God promised to the Hebrew people. With his wife Sarah he moved from place to place in the hills and wilderness plains of Judea. Their great sadness was that they had no son. At last God promised that a son would be born to them. They named him Isaac.

It was Abraham who established his people in the country which has been their spiritual home ever since his time. The Hebrews, or Jews, were later driven from it for many centuries, but they never forgot that for them it was the promised land.

One of Abraham's grandsons, Jacob, was the father of twelve sons, who gave their names to the twelve tribes of Israel.

Abraham also had a son by a slave woman named Hagar. The Bible tells us that Hagar and the boy Ishmael were driven away after Isaac's birth. Ishmael's descendants were the Arabs who lived in the southern wilderness. So Jews and Arabs trace their ancestry to the same great pioneer, Abraham. His journey from Ur to Canaan changed the history of the world.

Moses

*L*ong ago some of the Jewish people lived in Egypt. They were treated cruelly by the Egyptians, and forced to work at hard jobs.

The Egyptians did not want the Jews to have too many children. Sometimes they killed boy babies. So when Moses was born his mother put him in a basket, which she hid among the reeds by the river Nile. She hoped to keep him from being killed.

The king's daughter found the basket with the baby inside. She said that she would raise the child as her own. She hired Moses' mother to nurse him.

Moses grew up in the princess' household, and became the leader of the Jewish people. After many adventures he led them out of Egypt, across the wilderness, and back to the country which God had promised to them.

In all of human history, very few men or women have had so much courage and wisdom as Moses. He led his people in battles, refused to give up when they were all threatened by hunger and lack of water, and kept them firm in their faith in God. God used Moses to teach them laws and customs which are still the foundation of our daily lives: laws concerning the worship of the one true God; respect for parents and family life; honesty and kindness in our dealings with our fellow men and women. His life and his leadership marked a turning point in history.

Your routes to discovery: Exodus 2-3; 14; 19:16-20:17; 34; Deuteronomy 1-6

Gideon

*A*fter the death of Moses, Joshua led the Hebrews across the river Jordan into the land which God had promised to Abraham hundreds of years earlier. The country was called Canaan then, and the Hebrews had to fight their way in; but gradually they settled down. The twelve tribes lived separately, but they were united by their strong belief in one God.

Each tribe had its own leaders, or judges. The book of Judges tells the stories of these leaders, both men and women. Famous among them was the mighty Samson, who fought against the Philistines near a city which is still named Gaza.

Gideon was another great leader. When the Midianite army was threatening to conquer the Hebrews, God sent an angel to call Gideon. How could the scattered tribes fight this great army of invaders? Gideon decided to rely on a few brave men, not on numbers.

He chose just three hundred of the finest soldiers. The Midianite army was camped in a valley. Gideon divided his men into three bands of one hundred each. He waited until nighttime. Then quietly they took up their position on three sides of the valley.

Each man was told to carry a trumpet, and also a pitcher in which a lamp was concealed. They crawled closer and closer to the Midianite camp.

Gideon had told them, "When I blow my trumpet, all of you do the same. Then hold up your lamps, and shout as loud as you can: 'The sword of the Lord and of Gideon!'"

The Midianites panicked when this happened. They were confused by the sight of enemies on three sides. They had no idea how few there were. One direction lay open to them, and they fled as quickly as they could.

With leaders like Gideon and Samson the twelve tribes of Israel established themselves in their small country.

Ruth

*D*uring the time of the judges, the people lived in small towns and villages, depending on the land for their livelihood.

In a town called Bethlehem there was a terrible famine. To avoid starvation, a man named Elimelech led his wife Naomi and their two sons across the Jordan river to Moab. Jews and Moabites had been enemies, but Elimelech and his family were welcomed and treated with kindness. The two boys later married Moabite girls, named Orpah and Ruth.

Then trouble came to the family. Elimelech died, and so did his two sons. Naomi, Orpah, and Ruth were left widows, and Naomi was far away from her own people in Bethlehem. She decided to go back. Orpah and Ruth hated to see her go. They came with her to the river to say goodbye.

Then Ruth, who loved her mother-in-law very much, said: "I cannot stay here. I will come with you."

Orpah begged Ruth to stay in Moab, but Ruth's mind was made up.

"Do not ask me to leave you," she said to Naomi. "I will go wherever you go. Nothing but death will separate us."

Naomi and Ruth came to Bethlehem, tired and penniless. Naomi's old friends hardly recognized her. It was harvest time, and Naomi told Ruth to join the people working in the fields of Boaz, a rich kinsman of her dead husband Elimelech. Boaz soon saw that Ruth was very beautiful, and he heard of her devotion to Naomi. He made sure that they found food and shelter.

It was the custom among the Jews that when a woman was widowed the nearest male kinsman took her into his household. Boaz was in love with Ruth, and wished her to be his wife, but another man was the closest relative to Naomi and Ruth. One day, in the presence of witnesses, Boaz asked this man whether he meant to take Naomi and Ruth into his home. This man knew that Boaz was eager to marry Ruth, so he gave up his claim to be her protector. Boaz and Ruth were married.

This story was very important to the Jewish people. Boaz and Ruth were blessed with children. Their grandchild, Jesse, became the father of David, the best loved of all the kings of Israel. So the girl who had come from Moab with nothing but her character was never forgotten.

Your route to discovery—The Book of Ruth

Samuel

*F*or a long time Samuel's father and mother had no children. At last their prayers were answered and they had a beautiful son. They took Samuel to the church in their village. He lived there under the care of Eli, the priest, and helped him in his work.

Each year his mother brought him a new coat for his birthday. She was very proud of her son, and Eli praised his work.

One night Samuel dreamed that a voice called him by his name. He ran to Eli, and said: "Here I am, sir."

"I didn't call you, Samuel. Go back to sleep."

It happened again a few minutes later. A voice called, "Samuel!" But when Samuel went to Eli he said that he had not called the boy.

When it happened a third time Eli said to Samuel, "It must be God calling you in your dream. If you hear the voice again, say to him, 'Speak, Lord. Your servant is listening.'"

When the voice came to him again in his sleep, Samuel sat up and said these words. (In the old-fashioned and beautiful words of the Bible his words are: "Speak, Lord, for thy servant heareth.")

God told him that when he grew up he would be a leader of his people. Their ears would tingle with the words which God would give him to speak to them. Years later Samuel understood, when God called him to be a prophet to the Jews. A prophet is a mixture of a leader and teacher and preacher of God's word. Samuel was to be the first of many prophets who made God's will known to his people.

Your routes to discovery—1 Samuel 1 and 3

15

David

*D*avid's mother and father lived in Bethlehem. They had a big family, with seven sons. David was the youngest. He looked after his father's flocks of sheep, while the older sons were soldiers or farmers or merchants.

David was very clever at protecting the sheep from wolves and foxes and jackals. He had a sling, and could shoot a stone very straight and hard, to drive the animals away. He also made up songs, playing on pipes or a stringed instrument like a guitar.

Samuel was now a grown man, well known as a prophet and leader. The Jewish people were living in twelve separate tribes, each with its own towns and villages. Samuel was told by God to find a king to bring the twelve tribes together and make them one nation.

"Go to Bethlehem," God said to Samuel, "and find the family of Jesse."

Jesse was David's father. Samuel came to him and said, "God has sent me to see your sons."

Jesse called each of his grownup sons in turn. Samuel knew that none of them was the king he had been sent to find.

"Don't you have another son?" he asked.

"Yes, but he is only a boy, David. He is out with the sheep."

"Call him," said Samuel.

When David came, Samuel knew at once that he was the one whom God wanted as king of his people. Samuel blessed the boy, and said, "One day God will call you to do great things for our nation. Be ready!"

Your route to discovery—1 Samuel 16:1-13

David and Goliath

*D*avid's brothers went away with the army to fight against the enemies of the Jews. David was still a boy. His father and mother sent him with parcels of food for his brothers.

He found them very sad and upset. They were fighting against the Philistines, who had a giant soldier named Goliath. Goliath had given a challenge. He said that he would fight any man in the Jewish army who dared to stand up against him. But Goliath was so huge, and so heavily armed, that none of the Jews dared to fight against him. Not even the king, Saul, who was a strong man and very brave, would risk certain death by facing the giant.

David said to himself, "I could beat Goliath. I can hit him in the forehead with a stone from my sling."

He told his brothers. They thought he was mad to think that he could face Goliath. King Saul came by, and someone said to him, "This boy says that he will fight against the Philistine."

Saul asked David how he could hope to defeat the giant. David told him about his sling, and showed him how it worked.

"If I can hit a wolf a long way off, I can surely hit Goliath between his eyes."

Saul offered David his bronze armor, but David said that it would not fit him.

"It would only make me clumsy," he said. "All that I need is my sling. But pray for me. I must not miss with the first stone."

Then David called out to Goliath, "I will fight you."

Goliath looked at him in amazement. "What, a boy like you? Come here, little fool, and I will cut your head off."

But while Goliath was laughing, David fitted a stone into his sling and sent it whizzing toward him. It hit him between the eyes, and he fell down with a crash. Everyone was astonished, and the Philistines ran away in a panic.

Later David became king and built the city of Jerusalem. There are many stories about him in the Bible, and we still sing some of the songs which he wrote. The most familiar of these songs begins: "The Lord is my shepherd."

Your route to discovery—1 Samuel 17

Solomon

When King David grew old his sons quarreled bitterly. Who was to be the next king? One son, Absalom, fought against David, but was defeated. Before he died, David saw Solomon proclaimed as the one who was to follow him.

Solomon was a clever and ambitious king. People used to quote his wise and witty sayings, or proverbs. For example, he said to lazy people: "Look at the ants, you sluggards! (An old word for what we would call 'couch potatoes.') See how they work, and shape up!" And about money and possessions he once said: "You can be rich, and yet have nothing. You can make yourself poor, and yet have real riches."

He was famous as a judge. His best known case involved two women. They came before him, each claiming a baby.

One said: "We each had a newborn baby, and we were sleeping in beds next to one another. Her baby must have died in the night. When I woke up I had her dead baby beside me."

The other broke in angrily: "She is lying! It was her baby that died. This baby is mine!"

Solomon ordered his servant to bring a sword.

"There is only one baby, and two mothers. All we can do is to give each of them half a baby."

The servant was about to cut the baby in half when the first woman burst into tears.

"Don't kill my baby!" she cried. "Give it to her if you must, but do not kill it."

The other woman said nothing. Solomon knew that the first woman was telling the truth. She cared too much to let her baby die. He gave it to her.

Although he was a brilliant and successful ruler, Solomon was not loved by the people as David had been. He grew rich, and spent money on expensive stables for his horses and houses for his many wives. The common people were forced to work on these projects.

Solomon did build a great temple, which is described in the Bible. For hundreds of years it was the center of worship for the Hebrews.

Unfortunately he did not train his son Rehoboam to be a wise king after him. Rehoboam was a bad-tempered, unjust ruler. The kingdom which David had united broke apart after Solomon's death. Now the Hebrews lived in two separate kingdoms. They were never again as strong as David had made them.

Your route to discovery—1 Kings 3

Elijah

*I*n the southern kingdom of Judah David's family continued to rule. The kingdom in the north was called Israel.

One of the kings of Israel was Ahab. He was a weak man, but his wife Jezebel was strong-willed. She came from Tyre, where the people worshiped different gods and goddesses, not the one God in whom the Jews believed.

Elijah was called by God to stand up against Ahab and Jezebel. Like Samuel he was a prophet, or one who proclaimed God's word to the people. Jezebel hated him because he openly despised her worship of foreign gods. She was determined to kill him. She meant to force everyone in Israel to bow down to the gods in whom she believed.

Elijah warned Ahab that there would be drought and famine in Israel if he did not follow the true God. This made Jezebel even more angry. Elijah had to flee from the city of Samaria because of her threats.

The drought came. There was no rain and the crops withered. God told Elijah to go to Zarephath, where a widow would look after him.

Elijah came to the widow's house and asked her for water. She gave it to him; but when he asked for food she broke down in tears.

"I am just preparing the last of our food for myself and my son," she said. "The famine has left us starving."

"Don't worry," Elijah told her. "Bake a cake with the flour which you have left. I promise you that your barrel of flour will never be empty, and you will have oil for cooking."

Elijah was right. There was always enough for the three of them to eat.

Then suddenly the widow's son was sick, and seemed to be dying. She called Elijah and begged him to help. Elijah carried the boy to his bed and gave him the kiss of life. He began to breathe again, and recovered.

Now God told Elijah to go back and face Ahab and Jezebel. Ahab saw him approaching, and cried out: "So you're back! How dare you come here, when you are the source of all our troubles!"

"It is you who bring troubles upon our people," Elijah answered. "I have come to prove to you that your gods have no power, and to drive them out."

He made the priests of Jezebel's gods build a wooden altar, while he built another.

"Let each of us pray for fire to burn our altar," he said.

The priests of Jezebel prayed and prayed, while Elijah mocked them. "Pray louder!" he cried. "Perhaps your god is asleep."

Then, when they failed, he prayed quietly to the God in whom the Jews believed, the God of Moses and Samuel and David.

"Show your power, O God," he said, "so that your people may have faith in you."

Suddenly the wood on the altar caught fire, and the people gave thanks. Only Jezebel and her priests were angry. She was all the more eager to kill Elijah.

Elijah now promised Ahab that the rains would begin again. Soon the land grew green and the crops were rich. But Elijah had to flee once again to avoid the vengeance of Queen Jezebel. He went out into the wilderness, and God sent an angel to watch over him and feed him.

Jezebel grew more and more greedy for power and possessions. Next to one of Ahab's palaces was a vineyard owned by Naboth. Jezebel wanted to turn it into her herb garden. When Ahab asked Naboth to exchange the vineyard for other land, he refused.

"My family has owned that land for generations," he said. "It would be against God's will for me to give it up."

When Jezebel heard this she had Naboth murdered, and took the land for herself. Ahab was too weak to try to stop her, but Elijah heard of her crime and hurried to the palace.

Ahab trembled when he saw Elijah. He knew that God would punish him for Naboth's death.

"You will die in battle," Elijah told him, "and the queen will shed her blood here where she killed this innocent man."

Soon Ahab went to fight against the army of the Syrians. He disguised himself as an ordinary soldier, to avoid being singled out for attack; but a chance arrow struck him, and he died.

Many years later a rebel general named Jehu overthrew Ahab's son and made himself king. Jezebel's servants killed her, and her body lay in the place where Naboth's vineyard had been.

As for Elijah, he was remembered as the greatest and bravest of the prophets. The Jews believed that when it came time for him to die a chariot and horses carried him up to heaven in a whirlwind.

Your routes to discovery—1 Kings 17-19; 21

25

Naaman's Servant

*T*his is the story of a girl who saved her master's life.

She was a Jewish girl, who worked in the home of a great soldier in Syria. He was called Naaman, and was a general in the army.

Naaman became sick with leprosy, a terrible disease of the skin which was very hard to cure. He tried every cure, but still he grew worse.

One day the girl said, "Master, if you would go to Israel, and ask the prophet Elisha to heal you, I am sure that he would."

Naaman did not believe it, but was so desperate that he decided to try. He took rich gifts with him, although the girl had told him that Elisha would not wish to be paid to heal him.

At Elisha's house he was told by a servant, "Elisha is in the middle of his prayers. He cannot come out to talk to you; but he says that if you bathe seven times in the river Jordan you will be cured."

Naaman was angry and scornful.

"What good will that do? Why can't I go home and bathe in the rivers of Syria, which are much bigger? Have I come all this way for such stupid advice?"

But his servants persuaded him that he should at least try.

As soon as he bathed in the Jordan his skin was cured. Overcome with joy and gratitude, Naaman hurried back to Elisha's house. He offered him rich rewards of money and other gifts, but Elisha refused them all.

"Give your thanks to God, not to me," he said.

Naaman always remembered that it was his servant who had saved his life.

Your route to discovery—2 Kings 5

Ezekiel

We saw that Samuel and Elijah were prophets. They were followed in later centuries by other men and women who felt the call to preach God's words to their fellow Hebrews. Often they risked their lives by speaking out fearlessly.

The first prophets whose message survived in written form lived about seven hundred and fifty years before Jesus. Each of them gives a vivid picture of God, in very beautiful language. Who can forget words like these? "He shall feed his flock like a shepherd, and shall gently lead those that are with young" (Isaiah). "They shall beat their swords into plowshares, and their spears into pruning-hooks" (Micah).

A terrible disaster fell upon the Hebrew people about six hundred years before Jesus. An army from Babylon captured Jerusalem. The city was destroyed, and many of the younger people were led away as captives. This would have broken the spirit of most small nations, but the faith of the Jews who lived in exile actually became even stronger. This was partly because of the leadership of their prophets, who kept alive their loyalty to God. They taught them that suffering can make men and women stronger if they face it with courage.

One of these prophets was a priest named Ezekiel. He told the exiled Jews about a vision which God had sent to him. He had dreamed that God showed him a valley full of dry bones, something like the trash dumps which lie outside modern cities. God asked Ezekiel, "Can these bones live?" Then he told him to say to the bones, "Behold, I will cause breath to enter into you, and ye shall live." In Ezekiel's vision the old, dried bones came together into skeletons. Then flesh and sinews appeared upon the bones. Finally God called upon Ezekiel to breathe on the bones and pray that they might live.

You can imagine how words like these gave courage to men and women who might have given up all hope. Ezekiel's vision came true.

Babylon was conquered, and the king of Persia allowed the Jewish exiles to return to Jerusalem if they wished.

Some of them did go back. They found their beloved city still in ruins, and the people without leaders. They began to tackle the huge task of rebuilding.

Ezekiel is just one of the religious leaders who made the Hebrew people so different from every other ancient nation. They never had a large country or a powerful army, but they taught the world more about God than any of the mighty empires which arose and fell beyond their borders.

Your route to discovery—Ezekiel 37:1–14

Nehemiah

*T*his is the story of a generous king and a patriotic, unselfish Hebrew leader.

The Jews who returned to Jerusalem after the exile had neither the resources nor the will to rebuild the city. After the temple had been replaced by a new one—probably much less richly decorated than Solomon's temple—a kind of stagnation and despair set in. Recovery was slow and painful.

A Jew named Nehemiah was cupbearer to King Artaxerxes of Persia, hundreds of miles away from Jerusalem. The king treated him as a friend, and was concerned when one day he saw him red-eyed from weeping.

"What has happened to you, Nehemiah?" he asked.

"I have had terrible news from Jerusalem, the city of my people," Nehemiah said. "They are surrounded by enemies, and the city is still in ruins."

He never expected what came next. The king urged him to go to Jerusalem, and gave him letters which would allow him to get things done in the king's name.

In Jerusalem Nehemiah met with many difficulties. While the Jews were building the city walls they had to be ready to fight off their enemies; but Nehemiah's leadership enabled the work to be completed.

Nehemiah was a lovable person, with high ideals, and a man of action. He gave up a comfortable and privileged position at the king's court to take on a very dangerous, hard task. Every country needs people like Nehemiah, who put their loyalty to the community above their selfish needs.

Your route to discovery—Nehemiah 2

Jonah

*S*ometimes the Hebrew writers told stories like those which Jesus later used to make his teaching more vivid. The book of Jonah is one of these stories. It tells us an important truth, but it is not meant to be taken as literally true.

It is the story of a man who tried to run away from what he knew God wanted him to do. He found that it was not easy!

Jonah was a prophet or preacher. He lived comfortably with his family, enjoying his home and his work. He often heard stories about the Ninevites, who had always been enemies of his country. He hated those Ninevites!

Then Jonah had a dream which put an end to his comfortable way of living. God spoke to him, and said, "Jonah, I want you to go to Nineveh and tell those people about me."

Jonah woke up with a start. "Preach to the Ninevites?" he cried. "I can't do that, Lord. I hate those Ninevites!"

But Jonah had a second dream, in which God told him the same thing: "Go and preach to the Ninevites. They need to know about me. The only way to reach them is through love, Jonah, not through hate."

Jonah was so upset that he decided to run away. He went to the nearest seaport, and bought a ticket on a ship which was sailing for Tarshish, as far away from Nineveh as it was possible to go.

But when Jonah was asleep in his bunk in the ship, he had another dream. He seemed to hear God's voice saying to him:

> You can't keep running away, Jonah.
> It's not like Jonah at all.
> You can't keep running away, Jonah.
> If you run, you'll only fall.

Jonah was worried, but he went back to sleep.

Suddenly a great storm arose. The ship was in danger of sinking. The sailors woke Jonah up.

"Pray for our ship to be saved," they cried to him.

Jonah was miserable. "The storm has come because of me," he said. "I ran away from what God told me to do. Throw me into the sea! Then the ship will be saved."

The captain did not want to throw Jonah into the sea, but when the storm grew worse and worse he knew that he must do so. He told the sailors to cast Jonah overboard.

As soon as Jonah hit the water the storm stopped. Poor Jonah was sure that he would be drowned, but suddenly a huge fish opened its mouth and swallowed him.

For three days Jonah was inside the fish's belly, praying to God to save him. Then the fish threw him up on to the shore. God called to him again:

Jonah, I'm calling you.
Don't run away from me!

Then God told Jonah again, "Go to Nineveh!" Still very unwillingly, Jonah went.

He preached to the Ninevites about God. To his amazement they listened. They begged him to tell them more about God's love. Jonah found out that the Ninevites were not cruel monsters, as he had believed, but people just like his fellow Jews.

Jonah went home happy. He had done what he knew God meant him to do. That was so much better than running away and hiding.

But he never forgot that huge fish!

Your route to discovery—The Book of Jonah

Christian Scriptures

Jesus' Message of Love

Christmas. What a wonderful word! It makes us think of families coming together to celebrate, of carols and lights on trees, and of the exchange of gifts.

All this happens because a baby was born in Bethlehem to Mary almost two thousand years ago. God cared so much for the men and women and children whom he had created that he had to come and share human life, with all its joys and sorrows. Jesus was the link between God the Father and each one of us. He opened up God's love to all the people in the world.

Jesus lived in a simple home in a Jewish town called Nazareth. There he learned to be a carpenter. It was not until he was about thirty years old that he became a teacher and healer, knowing that this was the work which he had come into the world to do.

Jesus chose twelve men to be his closest friends and followers. Just as close to him were a number of loyal women. The twelve men went with him from village to village, teaching people about God, and showing them how they could change their lives by sharing God's love with others.

Ordinary people who met Jesus and listened to him felt the power of his love; but when big crowds began to be attracted by his teaching and healing it made the Jewish leaders nervous. If large numbers followed him so eagerly it might cause trouble in a country which had seen many outbursts of violence.

It was not the Jewish people who turned against Jesus. We must always remember this. His Jewish friends could not have been more loyal and courageous. A small group of frightened, angry men, including the high priest, had him arrested. They caused him to be cruelly put to death.

His followers were amazed and overcome with joy when he came back to them, risen from the tomb. He gave them fresh courage to carry his message of love out into the world.

The later books of the Bible describe how Peter, Paul and others did this. They went from country to country within the great Roman empire. They risked their lives to bring together new churches. These were not buildings like those which we know now, but the homes of faithful men and women who invited others in to share worship.

Jesus Goes to a Wedding

When Jesus knew that it was time for him to leave home and face the world, he prepared himself by going alone into the wilderness. As he prayed and fasted there he had a vision. Satan himself, God's enemy and the source of evil, seemed to be tempting him.

"You could do anything, Jesus," Satan said. "You could perform spectacular miracles and conquer the world. You and I together."

"You and I can never be together, Satan," Jesus replied. "Leave me alone!"

Now Jesus was ready for his work.

One of the first stories told about his ministry is about a wedding in a town named Cana, near Nazareth. Jesus and his mother were invited, and they went together.

It must have been a big wedding. During the party the bride's mother found to her horror that they were running short of wine. Mary saw what was happening. She already knew that her son Jesus had unusual powers of healing and love.

"Could you help them, Jesus?" she asked.

It seems from the words of the gospel of John that Jesus said to her what many sons might have said to their mothers: "Now, Mother, don't pressure me!" But we can be sure that he spoke lovingly.

Mary knew that he would help if he felt it to be right. Sure enough, her hopes were fulfilled.

Jesus asked the servants to fill six large jars with water. Then he said a blessing. The toastmaster had been worrying that the wine would soon run out. When he tasted a glass drawn from one of the jars he was astonished.

"This tastes wonderful!" he said. "At most weddings they serve the best vintages first, and cheaper wine later; but this is superb!"

Jesus never performed miracles in order to show off his power, but he found it hard to refuse his help when people were in any kind of genuine need.

You can draw three lessons from this story.

First, if you invite God into your home he will never refuse or say that he is too busy. So we try to make our homes a place where we are not ashamed for God to come in.

Second, when he comes he will sweeten and enrich the life of the people within the home. He can "turn water into wine" in many different ways. A home which welcomes him is a home full of rejoicing.

Third, a life lived close to God grows richer and richer. The toastmaster said that the good wine had been kept to the end of the party. That can be true for you and me also.

Your route to discovery—John 2:1-11

A Team of Friends

*N*obody can work alone, not even Jesus. He knew that he needed trustworthy friends to help him.

He was often in the fishing towns by the lake of Galilee. Fishermen who worked there did good business. They were self-reliant, hard-working people.

Early one morning Jesus saw four of them by the shore. They were mending their nets.

"Good morning, Simon," Jesus said to one of them. "How was your catch?"

Simon replied, "We had no luck. A bad night."

"Why don't you try again?" Jesus asked.

Simon and Andrew were tired. All they wanted was to go home and rest.

"Look, Jesus, there are no fish out there. You know about carpentry, I know the lake. It would be a waste of time."

"Not if you try the deep water," Jesus said.

There was something in the way he spoke which made Simon and Andrew decide to go out again. They never forgot what happened next.

As soon as they spread their nets in the deep water a huge catch of fish almost sank the boat. They had to call their friends James and John to help them. Shaken and astonished, they came to Jesus after they had hauled in the catch. "Master, I'm sorry," Simon began, but Jesus interrupted him. "I need you, all of you—Andrew, James, John. I need brave friends to go fishing for human souls. Will you come?"

They followed him from that day forward, and became his most trusted helpers. He chose eight others also—ordinary men from normal jobs, the kind whom God needs in every generation to do his work.

It is good to read that Jesus gave many of them nicknames, as often happens between friends. Simon was "Rocky" (that is what Peter means); Andrew's name means courageous or "Feisty"; James and John, with their quick tempers, were "The Thunderers"; there was another "Little James," to distinguish him from the first James, and another Simon, who may have been nicknamed "The Eager Beaver."

They are sometimes called disciples in the story of Jesus. That means learners. At other times they are called apostles, which means people sent out to preach. Each name fitted them well. They learned from Jesus, and went out fearlessly to spread the good news which he had taught them.

Your route to discovery—Luke 5:1–11

43

The Kingdom of God

One of the first and most important things which Jesus taught his followers was that if they joined with him they would become part of a kingdom.

"It is different from most kingdoms," he said. "We don't have crowns and palaces. It is a kingdom in which you can share now, and one which you can help to build. I do not promise you riches or the kind of power most kings seek. You will give up most of your possessions; but once you are truly part of my kingdom you will find happiness and fulfillment here and in the life to come."

He used many images to describe his kingdom. Here are two of them.

The kingdom of heaven is like a precious pearl. What would a gem merchant not give to possess such a jewel! But that pearl is not worth more to him than your part in the kingdom is worth to you. Owning money or possessions always leaves us greedy for more, but being close to Jesus and enjoying the wonderful love of God is a treasure too precious to calculate.

But the kingdom of heaven is also like a seed, Jesus said. When you plant it, it is tiny, but in the right soil, and with the right care, it will shoot up at incredible speed. He called it a mustard seed, because in his country mustard was a quick-growing tree. You and I are God's sowers, if we accept our place in the kingdom. If we work hard enough, it will be like the tree which he pictured, where all the birds of the air could make their nests. The kingdom will not be complete until every man, woman, and child is offered a place within it.

Your route to discovery—Matthew 13:31–32, 45–46

JESUS AS TEACHER

Jesus used many more stories in his teaching. These are some of them.

The Lost Sheep

A shepherd looked after a hundred sheep. At the end of the day he led them back to their fold. He counted them: "One, two, three," all the way up to ninety-nine. One was missing.

He shut the ninety-nine sheep in the fold.

"I will come back soon," he told them. Then he went out to look for the one lost sheep.

"Where are you, little one?" he kept calling.

At last he heard a faint "Baa."

"I can hear you," he cried. "Call again, so that I can find you."

"Baa," said the sheep, a little louder this time. Soon the shepherd found him. His wool was caught in the thorns of a bush.

"There you are! Not hurt? Good! Let's go home."

So he picked up the lost sheep, and carried him back to the fold.

Jesus told this story to remind us of two things. God never gives up on someone who is lost and needs his love. And he wants you and me to look for lost and lonely people—like lost coins and lost sheep—just as you would want someone to look for you if you were the one who was lost.

*Your route to discovery—*Luke 15:3-7

The Lost Coin

A woman who was quite poor had saved up ten silver coins. She knew that soon she would be able to find a better home for her family, and to buy more food.

Early one morning she was counting the coins by the light of a candle: "One, two, three ..." She came to "nine"—and the tenth coin was lost.

She called out to her husband to help her find the tenth coin. He was very angry because she had lost it. Some of the neighbors heard them shouting and came to see what was going on. Soon everyone was looking for the lost coin.

"Give me that broom," she said to her husband. She swept under a cupboard, and there was the coin.

"Thank God we have found it!" she said. "Let's all have a cup of coffee to celebrate."

Do you ever see someone at school who looks lost and left out of things? If you do, try to make that person feel wanted and loved. You can be like God's broom, finding lost people and bringing them back from loneliness.

Your route to discovery—Luke 15:8-10

49

The Sower

*I*n Jesus' time a farmer would scatter seed over his freshly plowed fields by hand. In this story the farmer was sowing wheat.

Some of the seed fell on the path at the edge of the field. The birds quickly ate this up.

Some fell in shallow soil on top of rocks. Because it could not put down deep roots, it soon withered.

Some fell in places where thistles grew beside it. The thistles surrounded it and prevented it from growing to its full height.

Some fell in good, rich soil. It produced a wonderful crop of wheat.

When Jesus' followers asked him to explain the parable, this is what he said.

"The field is my kingdom, which God has sent me to found here on earth. When I offer people the chance to be part of that kingdom, some do not take any notice. They are like the seed which fell on the path.

"Some are full of enthusiasm for a little while, but they have no roots. Soon they lose interest.

"Some try to grow close to God, but their good intentions are choked by other desires, like love of money or power.

"But some are like the good seed which fell on rich soil. One person like that can yield wonderful fruit, spreading love and joy to many other people."

Your route to discovery—Matthew 13:1–23

The Wedding Feast

*O*nce a king sent out invitations to the wedding of his son. He asked all the rich and powerful people in his kingdom to come to the celebration.

He became very angry when most of them refused his invitation. They made all kinds of excuses. It seemed that none of them was grateful for being asked.

The king decided to ask all the poor people instead. The blind, the deaf, the lame, the homeless: he invited all of them. Naturally they were delighted: a party at the palace!

As each one arrived he or she put on a white robe which the king provided. Then they went in to enjoy the feast. But one man did not bother to put on his robe. He pushed his way in, and began to eat and drink greedily, not caring in the least what the party was about. The king had him thrown out of the palace.

This was another of Jesus' stories about his kingdom. As he traveled from place to place he found that the rich and powerful often refused to listen to him. It was ordinary, simple people who came close to him and were grateful.

You and I can be part of the wedding feast, if we listen to Jesus' teaching and make it the foundation of our lives.

Your route to discovery–Matthew 22:1–14

The Good Samaritan

One day a man asked Jesus, "What are the most important rules to keep so as to live a good life?"

Jesus said: "You know what is written in your Bible: the old commandments, to love your God and love your neighbor."

"Yes," said the man, "but what does that mean? Who is my neighbor?"

So Jesus told him this story.

A rich merchant was traveling from Jerusalem to Jericho, along a steep, winding road where thieves often waited to rob people. Halfway along the road he was attacked, beaten, and robbed. He lay by the roadside, badly hurt.

Several people saw him as they passed, and heard his cries for help. They were too frightened to stop, so they hurried by on the other side of the road.

Then a foreigner came by, a man from Samaria. The Jews in Jesus' day did not like the people of Samaria, who lived just north of Judea—just as now some nations dislike and quarrel with the people who are their neighbors.

The Samaritan stopped to help, not worrying about the danger. He tied bandages on the man's wounds and lifted him onto his donkey. He took him to an inn which was close by. He paid for a room where the injured merchant could rest until he was better. The Samaritan promised to come back later so as to find out whether he had recovered, and to pay more money if it was needed.

"That is what 'loving your neighbor' means," Jesus said.

One of the things churches try to do now is to help hungry or homeless people when they ask for food or shelter. Because of Jesus' story, we often call unselfish people "good Samaritans."

Your route to discovery—Luke 10:25-37

54

The Prodigal Son

"*P*rodigal" is an old word used to describe people who spend money carelessly and waste their gifts.

Jesus told this story about a family: a father and mother and two sons. The elder son worked hard on his father's farm, and was very reliable. The younger was much more happy-go-lucky. He did things without thinking carefully first. Everybody liked him, but he was hard to keep under control.

This younger son (I suppose he was about sixteen) decided that he wanted to go out into the world and have some adventures. His father and mother could have stopped him by refusing to give him any money; but they decided that he would learn more by going and making his mistakes. They hoped he would soon want to come home again.

So he started out from home with a bundle of possessions and some money.

"My brother never sees what the world is like beyond our home farm," he thought to himself. "I am going to make my own way. Maybe I will become a sailor, or live in the city and earn a lot of money. Then I can go home and tell him all the things that he has missed."

For a few days everything went well. He was soon in towns that he had never heard of, and it was a little frightening to be among strangers. But he had money to buy food and lodging. It all seemed like a great adventure.

Then came disaster. While he was sitting in a cafe, with his bag by his feet, somebody stole it. In a flash he had lost everything, including his money. What was he to do? He went to a farmer and asked for work. "I'll do anything," he said.

The farmer was a rough, hard man.

He decided that this spoiled kid needed a lesson.

"You can look after my pigs," he said. "Feed them and keep the sties clean."

"What can I have to eat?" said the boy, who was very hungry.

The farmer laughed. "You can eat what they eat. Corn husks. You won't starve."

So the boy lived with the pigs, and grew dirtier and hungrier and more desperate every day.

"Why did I ever leave home?" he said to himself. "If only I could go back! But my father is probably so mad at me that he wouldn't want me. Still I must try."

He started out to find his way home. It wasn't easy. His shoes were worn through. He had to beg for food. At last he could see his home in the distance.

What he did not know was that his father and mother had missed him terribly. Every day they spent time on the roof of their house, watching the road to see whether he was coming back. One day his father thought he saw a lonely figure far away. He ran to fetch his wife.

"There's somebody out there," he said. "I can't recognize him yet, but it could be our son. I'm going out to see."

57

The father ran out into the road, and hurried toward the person he had seen in the distance. As he came closer he saw that it was his son—but how he had changed! He was thin and pale. His clothes were in rags. All of his smiling confidence had vanished.

"Dad!" called the boy, sobbing. He tried to run to this father, but he was too weak. He stumbled and fell. His father knelt down beside him.

"Son!" he cried, holding the sobbing boy in his arms. "Thank God you're home again!"

"You mean you will take me back?" the boy whispered.

"Take you back? We have been so worried about you. We prayed to God to look after you. Now come on in to your mother."

He had to carry the boy, because he was so weary and his feet were bleeding. The son kept murmuring, "I'm sorry, Dad, I'm sorry."

His mother was shocked when she saw him. She quickly prepared a bath, and found ointment for his cuts and bruises. Meanwhile his father told the servants to prepare a great feast for everyone in the house. He ran out to tell his elder son that his brother was home.

At first the elder boy was rather surly.

"So the prodigal has come home?" he said. "You're going to have a feast, are you? What about me? I work all the time."

His father embraced him. "I know how you feel," he said. "We love you too, son. You are the one who always helps us. But we were afraid that we had lost your brother. Come on, welcome him back! I'm sure that he has learned to live very differently from now on."

They all sat down to dinner, the family and the servants. Through this story Jesus was telling us that God's love never stops, even if we turn away from him. We can always come back and begin again. And if God treats us like that, we also ought to look for people who have made mistakes and found trouble. Sometime in your life you will need love and forgiveness, just as the prodigal son did, and sometime in your life you can help another person with understanding and forgiveness, as his parents helped him.

Your route to discovery—Luke 15:11–32

JESUS AS HEALER

It soon became known that Jesus had healed sick and crippled people. Naturally many more came to beg for healing, either for themselves or for their loved ones.

Jesus taught them that they could heal themselves if they had enough faith in God. What they needed, he said, was to be made whole in body and mind and soul. It might be paralysis or skin disease or mental illness which kept them sick. Others were sick with greed for money or with hatred or envy. Their sickness was in their minds and hearts. He tried to show each sick person or sinner the way to cure himself or herself.

A Woman in a Crowded Street

Once in a crowded street a woman touched the edge of Jesus' robe. She had been sick for many years, and she believed that even to touch this great healer might cure her.

Jesus immediately knew that this was not someone brushing against him by chance. He stopped and asked, "Who touched me?"

Peter began to say that Jesus could not possibly tell who touched him, when a crowd was jostling him all the time.

"No, this was different," Jesus said. "I felt power passing from me to another person. Was it you, lady?"

The woman, who was kneeling by him, nodded her head.

"Do you feel a change in your body?" he asked.

Then the woman, weeping for joy, told him that when she touched him the bleeding which had been going on for years suddenly stopped.

"You healed yourself because of your faith," he said.

There is such a huge difference between bumping into people in a crowd and reaching out to touch another person with love and faith.

Your route to discovery—Mark 5:25-34

A Man with Palsy

*I*n a place called Capernaum the word spread that Jesus was in a house. Soon crowds of people pushed their way to the house. Among them were men from Jerusalem, sent by Jewish leaders to find out who this healer was.

An amazing thing happened while Jesus was inside the house. Four friends tried to carry a man who was sick with palsy, or paralysis, through the door. Their way was blocked. There was an outside stairway to the roof. In desperation they lifted the sick man up. Then they tore a hole through the roof, and lowered him into the room below.

Naturally this caused a commotion. Jesus said: "Look how much faith this man and his friends have! Nothing could stop them."

He knew that the men from Jerusalem were watching him with suspicion. He said to the sick man: "You can make a fresh start, my friend. Your sins are forgiven."

The men began to mutter among themselves. "You see? He cannot heal this man, so he pretends to forgive sins! As if he has power to forgive sins! Only God can do that."

Jesus knew what they were saying.

"What is it that worries you?" he asked. "Do you think it is easy to say, 'Your sins are forgiven,' and harder to say, 'You are healed'?" Then he put his hands on the sick man. "Your sickness is gone," he said. "You have wonderful friends."

Your route to discovery—Mark 2:1-12

"Be Opened"

*T*he friends of a deaf man, who also had an impediment in his speech, brought him to Jesus in Galilee. Jesus drew the man aside so that he could talk to him quietly.

In Jesus' time many people believed that if a healer spat on his hand and then touched a sick person, the cure was more likely to be effective. Jesus knew that if he did this the man would be encouraged to believe that he was being cured. So Jesus first touched the man's deaf ears, then spat and touched his tongue.

Then he prayed, and said to the man: "Be opened! You can hear and speak!"

The man began to hear. It was such a new experience that at first he was confused, but Jesus told him that soon he would be accustomed to hearing.

"You are going to speak and hear just like other people," he said.

So the man ran back to his friends rejoicing.

Your route to discovery–Mark 7:31-37

Ten Lepers

One day Jesus met and healed ten lepers.

Leprosy is a disease of the skin. Now it can be treated by doctors and cured.

In Jesus' time there was no cure. Most people were so frightened of catching it that they would not go near a leper, even if he or she were one of their family. These poor people were driven out of the villages to find their own shelter in the countryside. Food was left for them to pick up.

A leper's only hope of returning to normal life was that the disease would cure itself. Then he had to ask a priest to inspect him and declare that his skin was clean.

Jesus showed no fear when he met lepers. (Other wonderful people have been the same, like Saint Francis, Father Damien, and Mother Teresa.) One day he met a band of ten together. They had heard that he was close by. They ran toward him, pleading to be healed.

"Your faith is healing you now," he said. "Go and ask the priest to verify that your leprosy has vanished."

They were so overcome with amazement and joy that they turned and ran, each eager to reach the priest first. Then a wonderful thing happened. One of them stopped, ran back, and knelt at Jesus' feet.

"Master, how can I thank you for what you have done?" he cried out.

Jesus found out that this man was a Samaritan, a foreigner, like the brave man who stopped to help a victim in the story of the good Samaritan.

"Only one out of ten came back to thank me," he said, "and he is not even a Jew."

I do not think that he was blaming the others. They were doing what he had told them to do, hurrying to find the priest. But he did think it a heartwarming thing that one had shown so much gratitude.

I wonder what happened to that Samaritan leper. Surely he must have gone home and told his family and friends about his amazing healing. Perhaps he became another sower, spreading the love of God.

Your route to discovery–Luke 17:11-19

FOLLOWING JESUS ON THE ROAD TO JERUSALEM

Zacchaeus

*A*fter three years of preaching and healing Jesus had become known all over Judea. The people who respected and loved him far outnumbered those who were jealous and hostile, but his enemies were powerful, and they decided that he must be killed.

He knew that it was very dangerous to go to Jerusalem at the time of the Passover, the most solemn feast of the Jewish year, but he believed that he must go there to carry God's message to the people.

He passed through Jericho on his way to Jerusalem. He needed to spend a night there, and there were plenty of people who would have been glad to ask him into their homes.

As he walked past a crowd of cheering people, Jesus looked up and saw the face of a man high up in a sycamore tree. In that face Jesus saw spiritual hunger. He knew that this man needed him.

"Won't you come down, friend?" he called to the man.

The people in the crowd were indignant.

"Don't talk to him, Jesus," they cried. "That is Zacchaeus the tax collector. He cheats us all to make himself rich, the swine."

Jesus took no notice.

"Zacchaeus, I need a place to rest. May I come to your home?"

Zacchaeus was overwhelmed. He had wanted to see Jesus, and because he was a very short man he had climbed the tree; but he had never expected to speak to him.

"Of course you may, Master," he stammered. "But—"

"Then let us go."

The people of Jericho were angry. Why would Jesus pick out a man like Zacchaeus to be his host? But that evening changed Zacchaeus' life. He promised to pay back all the money he had made dishonestly, and to give generously to the poor and the sick.

Zacchaeus would have liked to follow Jesus to Jerusalem and become one of his disciples. Jesus told him that he must stay in Jericho and go on doing his job.

"But from now on the people here will know that you are an honest man," Jesus said to him. "That is the way in which you can show them what God has done for you."

The next morning Jesus and his friends started out for Jerusalem. It was his last journey.

Your route to discovery—Luke 19:1–10

The Last Supper

On the last night of his life Jesus had supper with his twelve apostles. They borrowed an upstairs room from friends in Jerusalem.

They were tired and dusty from walking. Before supper Jesus told them to take off their sandals. He asked for a basin, a pitcher, and a towel. Then he went around the table, washing their feet.

Peter protested that he should not be doing it, but Jesus said: "This is how it works in my kingdom. The master is the servant. Always remember that when I am no longer with you."

They shared a simple meal. At the end of the meal Jesus blessed a loaf of bread and a cup of wine. "This is my body," he said, "and this is my blood. When you come together to remember me, do as we are doing tonight."

They all shared the bread and the cup.

That supper has been the model for Christians ever since. We meet and share bread and wine, knowing that they mean for us the love which Jesus showed toward his friends.

Your routes to discovery—Matthew 26:17-29; John 13:1-17

Jesus' Resurrection and Ascension

On Good Friday we remember the death of Jesus. His family and friends were overcome with grief when it happened.

On Easter Sunday we remember the resurrection. The same people who had been in despair at his death shared the glorious news that he was alive, and had spoken to Mary of Magdala when she went to tend his grave. At first they could hardly believe it, but for the next forty days he often appeared to many different people. They had no doubts left. He was alive.

One day he came back to the lake of Galilee. It was early morning. Seven of the twelve apostles were there by the shore.

Peter went out to fish, with James and John. They heard a voice calling to them from a distance.

"Have you caught anything?"

"Not yet," Peter answered. He did not recognize that it was Jesus.

"Try casting to your right side," Jesus said.

When they did this, it was a repetition of the morning when Jesus first called them to be his followers. A catch of fish filled their nets.

John shouted to Peter, "It is Jesus!"

Peter jumped into the water and raced to the shore.

Meanwhile Jesus had lit a fire. Once again they shared a meal, this time of bread and fish.

Each time they saw Jesus and talked to him it strengthened their belief. Now they were ready for him to say a final farewell.

He took them to a hill near Jerusalem, and spoke to them for the last time.

"Stay in Jerusalem," he told them, "and wait for the power of God's Holy Spirit to come to you. Then go out and proclaim God's love to all the world."

They never saw him again, but ten days later his promise was fulfilled. They were together in the room where he had shared that last supper with them. They felt a surge of power and joy, and knew that the Spirit had filled their hearts. It gave them the courage to do as he had told them.

Ever since then the story of Jesus' life has been told to people all over the world. If you believe in him, you too must share the good news. God needs you as much as he needed Peter and his other friends.

Your routes to discovery—John 21:1–14; Acts 1:1–12